W9-BFB-181

Monkey Business

SPIDER MONKEYS

Gillian Gosman

PowerKiDS
press
New York

Published in 2012 by The Rosen Publishing Group, Inc.
29 East 21st Street, New York, NY 10010

First Edition

Editor: Jennifer Way
Book Design: Kate Laczynski

Photo Credits: Cover, pp. 1, 5, 7, 8, 9 (right), 11, 12, 13 (right), 17, 20, 22 Shutterstock.com; p. 4 Ralph Hopkins/Getty Images; p. 6 Roy Toft/Getty Images; p. 9 (left) Thomas Marent/Visuals Unlimited, Inc./Getty Images; p. 10 Alfredo Estrella/AFP/Getty Images; p. 13 (left) David Tipling/Getty Images; pp. 14–15 © Animals Animals/SuperStock; p. 16 © Mason Fischer/Peter Arnold, Inc.; p. 18 Medioimages/Photodisc/Thinkstock; p. 19 Hemera/Thinkstock; p. 21 Frans Lemmens/Getty Images.

Library of Congress Cataloging-in-Publication Data

Gosman, Gillian.
 Spider monkeys / by Gillian Gosman. — 1st ed.
   p. cm. — (Monkey business)
 Includes index.
 ISBN 978-1-4488-5020-4 (library binding) — ISBN 978-1-4488-5173-7 (pbk.) — ISBN 978-1-4488-5174-4 (6-pack)
 1. Spider monkeys—Juvenile literature. I. Title.
 QL737.P915G674 2012
 599.8'58—dc22
                                        2011000664

Manufactured in the United States of America

CPSIA Compliance Information: Batch #WS11PK: For Further Information contact Rosen Publishing, New York, New York at 1-800-237-9932

Contents

MEET THE SPIDER MONKEY

Watch as a spider monkey wraps its tail around a branch. It reaches one long, thin arm out into the air. The monkey jumps and seems to fly before its feet touch down on another tree, 40 feet (12 m) away!

Spider monkeys get around by jumping, swinging, and bouncing through the highest branches. Their long arms,

Spider monkeys use their long tails to hold on to branches and balance in trees.

legs, and tails may make them look a little bit like spiders climbing through the trees, but these animals are **primates**, like you and me!

Spider monkeys have very flexible bodies. "Flexible" means "able to move easily."

5

MANY MONKEYS

There are several **species**, or kinds, of spider monkeys. All of these species have a few things in common. They all live in the same part of the world, in Central America and South America. They all have long arms, legs, and a tail, which are used for moving easily among the treetops.

This is a Geoffroy's spider monkey in Costa Rica.

A spider monkey's arms are long. They do not use their arms to help them walk. In fact, spider monkeys are one of the only monkeys that walk upright, on two legs!

Spider monkeys walk upright, but they spend more time swinging in the treetops than walking.

FROM THE NEW WORLD

Spider monkeys are **New World** monkeys, which means they live in Central America and South America. **Old World** monkeys live in Africa and Asia.

New World monkeys have **prehensile** tails. These tails are adapted for holding on to things tightly. They are used like extra hands and help the monkey swing from tree to tree.

New World monkeys are also known for their noses.

This black-handed spider monkey lives in Belize. Belize is a country in Central America.

They are longer and thinner than the noses of Old World monkeys. The New World monkey's **nostrils** are also set far apart and each face out to the side, rather than forward.

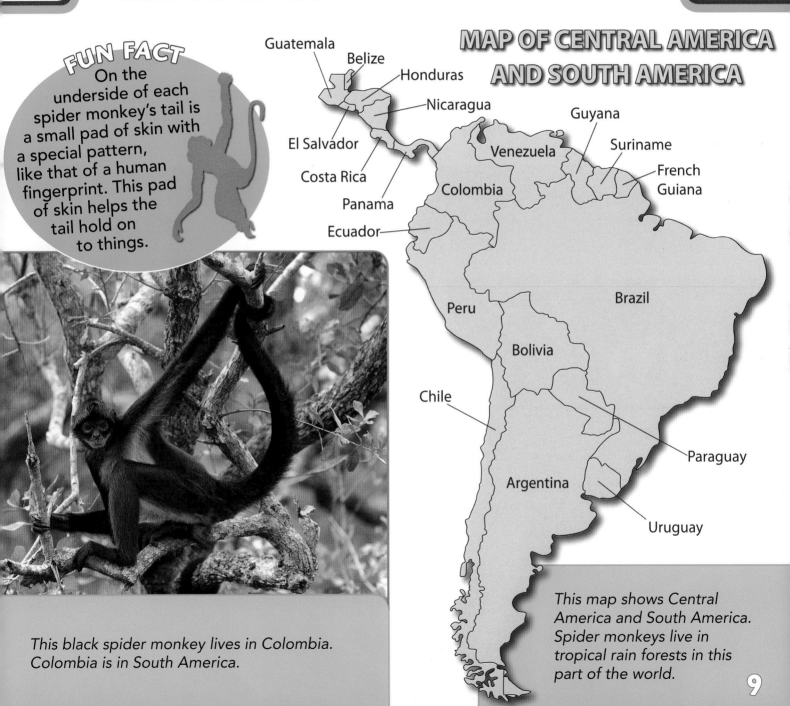

FUN FACT
On the underside of each spider monkey's tail is a small pad of skin with a special pattern, like that of a human fingerprint. This pad of skin helps the tail hold on to things.

MAP OF CENTRAL AMERICA AND SOUTH AMERICA

Guatemala
Belize
Honduras
Nicaragua
Guyana
El Salvador
Suriname
Venezuela
French Guiana
Costa Rica
Colombia
Panama
Ecuador
Peru
Brazil
Bolivia
Chile
Paraguay
Argentina
Uruguay

This black spider monkey lives in Colombia. Colombia is in South America.

This map shows Central America and South America. Spider monkeys live in tropical rain forests in this part of the world.

THE HIGH LIFE

Spider monkeys are found across Central America and in parts of South America. They live in thick, tropical rain forests. They are **arboreal**, which means they spend almost all of their time high in

This spider monkey lives in Nicaragua, in Central America. Here spider monkeys share their habitat with other monkeys, such as howler monkeys.

Spider monkeys often lie along branches because this makes it easier for them to stay balanced in the tree while resting or sleeping.

the treetops. They come to the ground only when the **canopy** is crowded with monkeys and food is hard to find.

The canopy is the highest layer of tree growth in the rain forest. Many small animals live in the canopy and the layers just below it. These parts of the trees are often between 200 and 300 feet (61–91 m) above the ground. There are strong winds and high temperatures up there.

TIME TO EAT!

Spider monkeys are **omnivores**. This means they eat many different things. Spider monkeys find their food in the rain forest canopy. They eat mostly plant parts, such as fruits, leaves, and nuts. They also eat insects and bird eggs.

Spider monkeys generally stop and eat

This spider monkey is using both of its hands to pick and eat food while hanging by its prehensile tail.

their food wherever they find it. They can eat while hanging by their tails. They can even eat while they are swinging between trees and while they are climbing from branch to branch!

Spider monkeys eat mostly fruit. When they cannot find fruit to eat, they will eat leaves.

Spider monkeys eat all kinds of fruits. This is a papaya tree, which grows throughout Central America and South America.

LIVING WITH THE MONKEYS

Spider monkeys are very social. This means that they like to spend time with one another. They spend their days playing in troops, or large groups. A spider monkey troop might have between 24 and 36 monkey members. At meals and bedtime, they go off in smaller groups of four or five monkeys. They stay in touch with the rest of the troop using calls and barks even when they are apart, though.

These Colombian spider monkeys have broken off from the others in their troop to rest together.

Female monkeys often lead troops and smaller foraging, or food-finding, groups. They decide where the group will look for food and take them to it.

BEDTIME FOR MONKEYS

When night falls, the smaller groups within a spider monkey troop go to different places. Each group finds a sleeping tree. A good sleeping tree is one that has high, strong branches. The monkeys are safest in the highest branches because **predators** such as jaguars cannot reach them there. The branches should be

This white-bellied spider monkey has found a comfortable and safe resting place high in the canopy.

forked, too, meaning they split in two. This makes a nice resting place for the sleeping monkeys.

If a predator does come during the night, the monkeys bark and act wild. If that does not scare the predator away, the monkeys run away. They do not put up a fight.

Jaguars live throughout Central America and South America. They eat many kinds of monkeys, including spider monkeys.

MALES AND FEMALES

Spider monkeys reach adulthood and can **mate** when they are about five years old. Between every two and five years, each adult female spider monkey picks a male monkey from her group for mating. The males and females are drawn to each other by their scents.

Male spider monkeys are a little bit bigger and heavier than females.

The baby monkey grows inside the mother for seven or eight months. When it is born, the baby's hair is all black. Its hair might change color over time, turning brown or red depending on the parents' hair color.

Here is a female spider monkey with her baby.

BABY MONKEYS

Baby spider monkeys stay close to their mothers for the first two years of their lives. For the first five months of their lives, they hold on tightly to their mothers' chests. Then they begin to ride on their mothers' backs.

You can tell that this Colombian black spider monkey baby is more than five months old because it is riding on its mother's back instead of on her chest.

As spider monkeys grow, they begin to play with other young monkeys and explore on their own.

Until they are two years old, baby spider monkeys drink their mothers' milk. As the young monkeys grow, they begin to play with other young monkeys and to learn about the world around them. When they are four or five years old, spider monkeys are fully grown.

FUN FACT

In the wild, spider monkeys can live to be more than 20 years old and grow to weigh about 20 pounds (9 kg).

PEOPLE PROBLEMS

Humans pose the greatest danger to the spider monkey. Some people hunt them for food.

Deforestation destroys the spider monkey's habitat. This leaves the monkeys with nowhere to live and find food. When this happens, the groups die out.

Some scientists think that the numbers of spider

The Colombian black spider monkey, shown here, is critically endangered.

monkeys of all species are going down. People have put spider monkey species on watch lists, or lists of animals that may become **extinct**. These watch lists help tell people about the problem and are helping to save the monkeys and their habitats.

Glossary

arboreal (ahr-BOR-ee-ul) Having to do with trees.

canopy (KA-nuh-pee) The highest tree branches in a forest.

deforestation (dee-for-uh-STAY-shun) When most of the trees in a forest are cut down.

extinct (ik-STINGKT) No longer existing.

mate (MAYT) To come together to make babies.

New World (NOO WURLD) North America and South America.

nostrils (NOS-trulz) The openings to the nose.

Old World (OHLD WURLD) The part of the world that includes Asia, Africa, and Europe.

omnivores (OM-nih-vawrz) Animals that eat both plants and animals.

predators (PREH-duh-terz) Animals that kill other animals for food.

prehensile (pree-HEN-sul) Able to grab by wrapping around.

primates (PRY-mayts) The group of animals that are more advanced than others and includes monkeys, gorillas, and people.

species (SPEE-sheez) One kind of living thing. All people are one species.

Index

A
arm(s), 4, 6–7

B
branch(es), 4, 13, 16

C
canopy, 11–12
Central America, 6, 8, 10

F
food, 11–13, 15, 22

G
ground, 11

H
hands, 8

K
kinds, 6

L
layer(s), 11
legs, 5–7

N
noses, 8–9
nostrils, 9

O
omnivores, 12

P
people, 22
predator(s), 16–17
primates, 5

R
rain forest(s), 10–11

S
sleeping tree, 16
South America, 6, 8, 10
species, 6, 22
spiders, 5

T
tail(s), 4–6, 8, 13
tree(s), 4–5, 8, 11, 13, 16
treetops, 6, 11
troop(s), 14–16

W
watch lists, 22
winds, 11

Web Sites

Due to the changing nature of Internet links, PowerKids Press has developed an online list of Web sites related to the subject of this book. This site is updated regularly. Please use this link to access the list: www.powerkidslinks.com/monk/spider/